★ AMERICAN ★
NINJA
WARRIOR

A BRIEF HISTORY

T0364066

Hachette Book Group supports the right to free expression and the value of copyright. The purpose of copyright is to encourage writers and artists to produce the creative works that enrich our culture.

RP Minis®
Hachette Book Group
1290 Avenue of the Americas, New York, NY 10104
www.runningpress.com
@Running_Press

First Edition: May 2023

Published by RP Minis, an imprint of Perseus Books, LLC, a subsidiary of Hachette Book Group, Inc. The RP Minis name and logo is a registered trademark of the Hachette Book Group.

The publisher is not responsible for websites (or their content) that are not owned by the publisher.

ISBN: 978-0-7624-8270-2

Contents

INTRODUCTION

If you're watching an athlete struggle to climb a cargo net or hang onto a giant log as it jolts down an uneven track, then hear fans start chanting for the athlete to "Beat that wall!" you can only be watching one show—*American Ninja Warrior*.

The hit show has captivated audiences for over thirteen years with some of the most incredible fitness feats and endurance trials ever seen on TV. Competitors run obstacle courses in various cities for the chance to make it to the final course. Each year, those Ninjas who have passed the qualifying rounds travel to the finals. At stake? A prize of one million dollars and the bragging rights of winning *American Ninja Warrior*.

The format is simple enough, even if the courses aren't! Different cities around the nation host the City Qualifier rounds. Ninja courses are built, and year after year, over seventy thousand people apply to get on the show. Many wait—camped out for days—to get through the walk-on process. While the walk-ons now use a lottery system, the wait is no less intense.

Once applicants are selected, the real test begins. Competitors must make it through a City Qualifier round, which contains six obstacles. The run is timed, so making it to the final buzzer isn't enough— Ninjas have to be quicker than their competitors! The top thirty Ninjas who complete the course with the best times are then able to run the City Finals course, which adds four more obstacles to the initial six.

The top fifteen contestants from each City Finals course then move on to the Finals. All the Finals, except for one season, have always been held in Las Vegas. The final course has four stages, and the final stage is known as Mount Midoriyama. With an incredible twenty-three obstacles divided among the four stages, and then the challenging seventy-five-foot rope climb up Mount Midoriyama, it's no wonder only three people have ever made it to the top, and only two have claimed the million-dollar prize.

So what does it take to be an American Ninja Warrior? Most Ninjas will tell you that a never-say-die spirit is the most important thing, meaning you should never give up. While that's true for such a grueling competition, physical fitness is also key. Speed, endurance, and grip strength are critical components of the sport. Grip strength can make or break a competitor on the course, so it's no surprise that many top Ninjas are from the rock-climbing world.

For many fans as well as Ninjas, the Ninja Warrior way has become a lifestyle. While athleticism is a core component, simply lifting weights and doing some extra cardio aren't going to get a Ninja to the buzzer. On the surface, an obstacle course may not sound as difficult as, say, the Olympics. However, the training and athletic ability needed to complete the various stages of the competition are intense.

NINJA HISTORY

American Ninja Warrior was inspired by a Japanese television show called *Sasuke*. The G4 network would broadcast dubbed episodes of the show in America. The network held annual contests called *American Ninja Challenge*, and the top challenge contestants would go to Japan and compete in *Sasuke*. The format proved so popular that *American Ninja Warrior* was born. They eventually moved the Finals from Midoriyama Studios in Japan to Las Vegas.

Since 2009, *American Ninja Warrior* has been a ratings blockbuster, at one point reaching 6.5 million average viewers. As the show became more and more popular, one regular season wasn't enough for Ninja

AMERICAN
NINJA
WARRIOR
2021

fans. Several All-Star editions have aired, where a select team of Ninjas compete against each other. There's also a special *Celebrity Ninja Warrior* edition that features celebrities running the course for charity; *American Ninja Warrior Junior,* designed for kids ages nine to fourteen; and three seasons of *American Ninja Warrior: Ninja vs. Ninja*, which pitted teams of Ninjas against each other.

Beginning in 2014, a global competition, *American Ninja Warrior: USA vs. the World*, featuring teams from different countries, kept the excitement going. The phenomenon isn't just limited to the US, either. Ninja Warrior shows are watched all over the globe: Australia, the UK, France, Germany, and many other countries.

NINJA VOCABULARY

//

Since the show debuted, certain words and phrases have now become part of the *American Ninja Warrior* vocabulary. A few of the most-familiar terms include:

» **Buzzer:** The buzzer is located at the end of each course (or stage), and a Ninja's time isn't final until they hit the buzzer.

» **"I see you!":** *ANW* host Akbar Gbajabiamila often inspires competitors when he points out seeing their efforts on the course.

» **Laché:** As in gymnastics, many obstacles require a swinging buildup of momentum to go forward.

» **Mount Midoriyama:** The fourth stage of the Finals, which includes a seventy-five-foot rope climb, straight up.

» **Ninja Killer:** Not a stealthy assassin, but an obstacle that proves so tough, most competitors can't get past it.

» **Switch Grip:** Grasping a bar with one hand facing forward and the other facing backward.

» **Veteran:** A Ninja who has competed on the show multiple times.

» **Keeping the Ls:** To cross many of the upper-body-focused obstacles, a Ninja needs to lock their arms in a 90-degree L-shape to conserve strength.

COURSE OBSTACLES

Over the years, certain obstacles have become fan favorites. The City Qualifying courses usually include some of the mainstay obstacles, rotating new ones in from city to city. Some of the toughest obstacles are known as Ninja Killers since they take out more than their fair share of Ninjas during competitions.

While athletes may expect certain obstacles—like the Floating Steps that almost always start the courses, where Ninjas must leap from side to side to reach each step—even veteran Ninjas have been taken out by obstacles they may overlook as easier than the Ninja Killers. On the course, as in life, it's best to pay attention! Some of the most popular obstacles include:

» **Jumping Spider:** Ninjas must leap up and plant both hands and feet against the narrow, vertical walls and inch forward without falling.

» **Wingnut Alley:** A Ninja Killer, contestants must swing from one wingnut-shaped ledge to another with precision timing.

» **Spinning Log:** Ninjas must race across a cylinder that spins without losing their balance and falling off.

» **Salmon Ladder:** Ninjas must use explosive strength to perform these leaping pull-ups.

» **Ring Toss:** Ninjas use the rings to swing and grab onto the next peg without losing their grip and falling.

» **Unstable Bridge:** Another Ninja Killer, contestants must use their grip to hang and "hop" forward along a plank, then swing across to a second plank and repeat.

» **Mount Midoriyama:**

While Stage Four sounds deceptively simple, it isn't—especially after completing three extremely challenging stages before tackling Mount Midoriyama. The seventy-five-foot rope climb straight up might be doable for many Ninjas when they are still fresh, but after completing all the other obstacles, it's an endurance test like no other.

BEAT THAT WALL!

Perhaps the most iconic obstacle in *American Ninja Warrior* history is the Warped Wall. Contestants must start from a short runway and some-how find the momentum to run up the fourteen-foot curved Warped

Wall. At the top, they must pull themselves up and over the ledge and hit the buzzer to stop their time. This would be difficult enough for most people—however, in 2016, the producers added six more inches to the Warped Wall, heightening the challenge.

Ninjas get three tries at the Warped Wall, and crowds quickly adopted the chant of "Beat that wall!" to inspire the athletes. This obstacle has claimed the run of many Ninjas to the point where many fail to scale it. The first female Ninja to beat the wall was Kacy Catanzaro, in 2014. Since, many more Ninjas have overcome this iconic obstacle.

Season ten saw the introduction of the Mega Wall, which is an incredible eighteen feet high. Ninjas are allowed one try at this wall, and if they fail, they have one shot at the regular Warped Wall. Ninjas who make it up the Mega

Wall receive a $10,000 prize. Later seasons allowed three attempts, with diminishing amounts of prize money, but the original one-shot attempt at the Mega Wall has since returned.

American Ninja Warrior, like its Ninja competitors, shows no sign of slowing down. A new generation of Ninjas has grown up watching the show and training for it, hoping for their chance to make it onto the show to complete the course.

It's likely Ninjas will hear the chant of "Beat that wall!" for many years to come.

This book has been bound
using handcraft methods and
Smyth-sewn to ensure durability.

The box and interior were
designed by Mary Boyer.

The text was written
by Chip Carter.